COFFEE POEMS

A POETRY COLLECTION IN FOUR VOLUMES

BY

WILLIAM SHIER

2020

For me

Truth may seem, but cannot be;
Beauty brag, but 'tis not she;
Truth and beauty buried be.

> - William Shakespeare, 'The Phœnix and the Turtle'

ABOUT THE AUTHOR

William Shier is a young writer from South-East England. He studied at Sussex University, earning both a bachelor's degree in English Literature and a master's degree in Literature and Philosophy. Currently, he is working on a novel and considering a return to academia for a PhD.

ACKNOWLEDGEMENTS

This series of poems began life during Prof. Keston Sutherland's 'Writing Poetry' module during the second year of my English Literature BA, in 2017. Sutherland's teaching and feedback have been invaluable for my development as a poet. This collection would not otherwise exist if I had not taken his units.

Furthermore, as part of the aforementioned module, I received copious, astute feedback from my feedback partner Freya Marshall Payne, who covered the hitherto written 'coffee poems' and other poems not included in this book. As with the feedback I received from Sutherland, Freya's letter was illuminating and encouraging. Much of this collection, however, was written following the completion of 'Writing Poetry' and has, until now, been read only by myself.

Thanks is owed to Frank O'Hara's *Lunch Poems* because the practice of composition behind that collection was a major inspiration for my method of composing *Coffee Poems*.

A different version of 'Volume I' formerly appeared on the website www.corrugatedwave.com.

Ultimate acknowledgement and thanks must go to my mother.

CONTENTS

VOLUME I – POUR 1

    Coffee with Foucault 2

    Coffee with Kiest – redacted 4

    Coffee with James 7

    Coffee with Gissing (and Derrida) 8

    Coffee with Rhys 11

    Coffee with 146923 (and Shakespeare) 13

VOLUME II – SIP 15

    Coffee with Marshall Payne (and then others) 16

    Coffee with Hopkins and F---- and N-------- 19

    Coffee with Huysmans 21

    Coffee with Barthes 24

    Coffee with A. Abbott 25

    Coffee with Beckett 28

    Coffee with Conrad 30

    Coffee with Leiris 32

VOLUME III – SWALLOW 34

    Coffee with Allison 35

    Coffee with Machine Number: 5239 36

Coffee with Bowen and S--------- 37

Coffee with Kenner 39

Coffee with Rose 40

Coffee with Lawley 43

VOLUME IV –EMPTY **46**

Not Caffeine 47

Whisky with Greenblatt (and Shakespeare) 50

Whisky with J. Paul 52

An Irish Coffee with Joyce 55

VOLUME I – POUR

COFFEE WITH FOUCAULT

The Shierean revised its head again
Though none named the way this time

Am I too fat
    too skinny
Probably too flat
Someways big
Someways minnie
Do I go on too long
Am I too quiet
Too loud
Quite, or too sl(e)ight
Do I dominate the convo
When id much rather submit

Too obscure
But not artistic enough
I haven't rolled in sauce
I wish I knœw
As much as the ones I aspire to
-the ones I read and write
-the ones I assay and test
-the ones I'm tested on
Or hardly anything at all

I'm stuck between dictions

- Not poetic enough
    in expression
- Not prosaic enough
    in clarity
- Not lyrical enough
    in flow

I'm stuck between
        worlds
            and people
                and places
                    and pages
                        thoughts
                            faces
                                hopes
                                    attempts
                                        and pains

It could have been coffee with others but no one was there and nobody came.

WILLIAM SHIER

COFFEE WITH KIEST – REDACTED

        Stationary camera,
        Painting in a corner facing outwards,
        No one else can see the canvas,
        Camera eventually pans 'round
        To show it.
        Is he mad?
        Is it blank, or black, or Brown,
        Does it look like white noise?
        Is it of himself or a lover?
        [Un]fortunately I cannot paint.
        I have decided it is brown white noise.
        Brown for the subtractive colour.
        The non-black white noise
        For everything else.

        A pheasant was crossing the train tracks home.

'Eat your pheasant, drink your wine,
your days are numbered, Bourgeois Swine!'

              'Oh but I like pheasant, my Grandma is given them'.
Then off to the gulag,
I thought.
I'm only being ironic,
Of course, of course.

        Scattered stuffing fluff along the park path,
        Teddy stuffing – blood, guts, gore – the ground.
        I was on the ground, id been on the floor.
        The journey back was always shorter.
        I hate the travel, it lengthens my day,

Without it though I wouldn't cool off,
And then theyd know and then itd be real.
But then they know now, this is a reflex,
The old way, and still I jump to it,
So used to my circles of suffering,
To Patterns of Dialogic Expression.
I do not mean to invent terms this time,
They are much more vulgar when I intend.
Twosand words in one night, four hours sleep,
And doubts ill ever seek learning again.
Complexity is too intense for me.
I hate the phrases that justify faith,
But ignorance would be bliss to me now,
And I would rather not know my devil,
The daemon that steals after me all day,
My most unentangled particle-ist,
Which is my most man-as-an-island-ist,
Which of course is all of everyday.
Me llorando, llorando, llorando.
O, sounding so edgy ive tripped and tipping,
Edging into another dimension.
You know my skin was tingly on the train,
No not specific addressed object
      only new ,

Although   .
Well   they're both older than me,
Unless   a sentence   .
   my skin trying for the expulsion
I prohibited my eyes from making.
         genre now?
Whilst know unmet criteria
  will prevent participation.
So, let me be clear
      both .

The essay wasn't great,
It was better   of   .

Where did all this come from?
And how did we get here?
Where will it go?
No one seemed to notice
That a verse of
Empilled
The message.
But when   ,
And loved his other songs
I questioned if I should have

Now   entertain   others,
     worse.

We're   ,
     feelings   no matter.

COFFEE WITH JAMES

My Dad asked me for help
Writing a personal statement.
When I wrote my uni one
He asked where id copied it from.
People expect expertise of me
But the more I learn
The less certain I am.
The more I write
The less I understand
 what a sentence is
I'm always asking for help
But I'm still expected to give advice

And then the sun came out
So lazy
I did that years ago
Though only to a few
In a different way
I'm in as the sun is out

So many sitting on the grass
With the gloss of a prospectus

Caffeine
Nicotine
I mean
Id rather have
Morphine
Or benzodiazepines
Have I been dirty enough to be clean

Sad songs don't make as much sense in the sun

COFFEE WITH GISSING (AND DERRIDA)

Or Voiced Through

I accidentally wrote a sonnet
Last night when I couldn't sleep.
I was thinking,
The pre-sleep fantasising haze
Mingling with awkward regrets
And tinged by the knowledge of an early start.
I thought of what I could write,
And then I had to write.
I wrote what I would write of their beauty.
The lines are as ugly as the poet.
Without realising I arrived at the couplet.

I want to write a crown of them
But not with that subject.
I just wanted coffee
But ex-family were in the way.
Unlike them I only have paper as company.

I hate that I wrote it.
Other than the bedside convenience,
That is why it's in the black notebook.

I remember my father
Buying a giant multipack of cigarettes,
All cellophaned together,
In duty free,
So he could survive the week
By slowly poisoning himself.
Now I'm not one to talk,
But I was then.

I leave my notebook unattended
And hope I find something new in it when I return.

I'm waiting for that second puberty,
That second batch of maturity.

Have you ever misheard some song lyrics?
But where you thought the singer sung something
More beautiful than the actual utterance?
…
> The sound of iron *shards* is stuck in my head,
> The thunder of the drums dictates
> The rhythm *often* falls *to* number of *dead*
> The rising of the *hearts* ahead
>
> From the dawn of time to the end of days
> I will have to run away
> I want to feel the pain and the bitter taste
> Of *your* blood on my *leaves* again
> …
> I can't *recall* your eyes, your face

Perhaps not more beautiful
But I imagine you understand.

I do not like measures that try
To add fondant to a burnt cake.
The thing with a burnt cake,
Assuming you're still hungry,
Is either that you eat it
Or you bake a new one.
The latter I insist on.

I try to read myself to sleep.

I read over the sonnet
And it has no turn

Just a brief detour and re-turn

It snows every night in Brighton
On those already too white
And entitled,
Some might say.
So many flounder like kites
And fly like beached whales.

If there was time I'd write a
Hate and Masturbation poem

"Scar tissue is stronger," I tell myself.
Later,
       I realise
              I'm wrong.

COFFEE WITH RHYS

The Lighght comes through the 4th story windows
And lighghts my table in the hallway.
It was there, empty, for me.
Or really for anyone else
Who could have sat there.
There are two chairs,
Pururple and Blueue,
I sit in Blueue.
The Lighght blinded me above table heighght,
So all the passers-by,
Contrastingly backlight,
Were figures to me,
Faceless voices.
Gumless teeth.

His paling eyes
From the blue of mine
to grey
His hair likewise
From the jet black
Darker than the dark brun of mine
To the grey of

I come back to my table
And there's a guy sitting in Pururple.
He hasn't written in my notebook,
Or read for me.
He gets up and leaves as I sit back down,
Then pauses as he walks away,
He vacillates,
Then sits down again.
It's okay that you were there.
You don't need to leave.

Not a heroine
The heroin

Oh, immoral English

COFFEE WITH 146923 (AND SHAKESPEARE)

The pink blossom of three trees,
The species I know not,
Has their petals, or leaves,
Scuttle across the steps
To the tune of the sombre song
On my headphones.

"Does anyone have a chainsaw?"
"Nifty versification".
"Perfect" "closure",
Closing itself again and again.
But the lines!
Parts connected by
Pinned red thread.
"Escapes freeness".
"Troubled with language".
What is its death wish?
Deliberately staged
[not staged by accident].
A found signature.
"Sputtering to silence".
"Professorial voice",
"Like a Radio 4 educational
programme".
The Four Quartets,
[I haven't read].
What if I were to tear
It down
This way?
It would feel like a mutilation.
[No, no, please do that].

I edit it more
That that
Discussed more

Aforementioned alterity
Clauses asyndeton
Nevertheless
The legastic self

You should take
"a few days" break.
"You're a born academic".
Thanks
But I'm made
And making
To make

"Excellent!".

The next person didn't arrive
So I had their time too.

Will it transcend expectations?

13

A tall ginger women walked past
Pulling beer and cakes behind.
I clearly missed the perfect meeting.
Instead I went where ex-family was.

"It's hard to make people say,
These days,
'What was that?'"
"You're so extra"

Volume II – Sip

COFFEE WITH MARSHALL PAYNE (AND THEN OTHERS)

Stir stick for the sugary drink.
Me with bitter bean juice.
It's louder here than I like.
The next Cambridge group?

I ripped it up
As I did before.

I'm extra and meta now.

Did I take the time for myself again?
The time as mine.

Knowing what one sees as beautiful
But not replicating it.

I left this alone
And it did not grow.
At least it's not the sonnets
That insist on shrinking.
But at least they end. gg

If I was part of a new group,
Where members know each other
And are known for themselves,
Who would I be?

I can't linger on these things anymore.
I don't care for my heritage.
Invariably I am legacy
And they are how I'm here.

I care about our inheritance
The
    texts.

The sun was naked
But now the day is dressed in grey.
Don't my sunglasses look silly.

The wine and pizza?
Not to whine but
The timing is conveniently inconvenient.

There's no whisky left for when I get back.
I'll have to eat instead.
Maybe washing down two pills a day
With cold tea
Will make me better at swallowing.

"I would like to see
'you' as literature -"
"Absolute
sentiment yet
many
    reworkings:
    a strange
    tension"

'Life is a performance, darling.'
Said before my least memorable performance.

Forearm sweat on the desk,
Like the residue of energy,
Like their lipstick on the lip of the top of the takeaway paper cup
Drunk 'in' though always taken away we
Remark on our conformity to the course
And how none of us are born to be.

The preface should illuminate,
How language has always been veiled?
It was a puzzle for me
And one I hated solving
And yet
Now I look for the near unsolvable,
It's what I know.
Clarity is uncomfortable.
Confusion is my nature.

COFFEE WITH HOPKINS AND F---- AND N--------

O absenthee, absenthee, absenthee;
O leave off, step away, forget release.

I do not kneel for a god.
I do not kneel for me.
I won't salute commanders.
I won't salute thee.

Nice to see
The identity
And identifying of different MEs
But not so nice to be

The LOWER CASE 'aitch'
Might not mean HIM,
As you sing a hymn,
But leaves the chance
- The mirrored male 'I'.
                  'his entire life in a nut shell'
                                  'in a nut shell'

Bitter to endure

As restrained as trellised ivy
And faithful as nettles

Directing their care too to what has no practical value
Ah yes, using the useless
                Civilisation

Order as compulsion.

The road to perfection isn't paved with bars of soap
he is dead and so am i
she is not dead and neither am I
we were never born

Transcription notation:
'practical' searched as 'preaxial' or 'phratral'
Read as 'preatrail'.

COFFEE WITH HUYSMANS

'Beyond the confines of time'
In the School of Business, Management, and Economics
The opposite,
                                                                What else?

Too many books to fit in with the food
So I put the thick one back

I said what I feared
And what terror meant to me
(the losing of identity
Or recognition of reality).
And others said loves,
For most of us at least,
From dogs to bods –
And all their fun products

Feeling fresh-eyed-and-eared
To a tasteless faceless place.
Lost in what has often been nearby
To study what I found some time ago.
Being offered welcome leaflets as comedy
When there's not long left to go.

'Alumni Spotlight'
Poorly lit
Does my school have such plaques?

What hate do I hold
Soon to be obvious history?
Precedent declares
There's something I'm missing.
But when I think,

There's only me

<u>With whisky</u>

We are of no elevation
Some even bring delumination

A feather pinned in a wooden stake
At the head of a flower bed.

Well,
    It wouldn't
        Be inevitable
            If it didn't happen.
            'O   rmet
            Ormot
            Amot
            About
            Armot'

'Truth cannot itself be true'

Do not faulter

I watch our poets on that programme,
Rip my pants off my person,
If this is their selection
For national television
Then I must be nothing.
The supposed *Avant-garde*
Only breaking from traditions long forgotten -
Exploding the unconstructed -
Fulfilling their own conventions,
Formulae and cliché.
I must be a pile of nothing.

I cannot find my notebook.
It's under printouts and pages

That I did not persevere with.
I slept for hours after minutes.
How could I ever hope to
Get ahead of those
Who thought
Of all the thoughts I live off.
The single thing I think of
Amot anymore,
The theses laid bare
In the volumes on page,
There throughout the ages,
That beat me to the punch.
When will I get ahead
Of those long dead?
I revolutionise?
I might survive,
Though I will be no-thing,
These words forgotten,
Never to ring
Off these voices that sing
Of the beauty of time
And the love of rhyme.

Once mind forgets __ type and kind,
Essence and rind, foul and ripe,
On off, one two, __ you,
3 and new, through and through,
Name and year, here and there,
Volume and worth, power and word,
Or------ utterance is irrelevant

COFFEE WITH BARTHES

There is no meaning which isn't desi ted — designated / disputed \ disputed

'Speak the word only'

Aural
Missing aural oral examination
When it's my specialisation
Glottal
Throatal
Aural, oral, throatal, glottal, guttural
Throttle down
              and
        in

ours theirs
The impossible infinitely intertwined idiolect
Unregulated communal usage

COFFEE WITH A. ABBOTT

Full all.
Except cup
And cranium
And lumbar.

The hubbub bubbles in the background;
A woven mesh the garment of silence.
Spikes in intelligence have long since
Landed flat to the death beep of mediocrity.

When there's no back to lean against
I must sit for myself upright.
Two hours before beginning I occupy my time
But I still feel late for my own earliness,
Early for everyone's lateness,
And on time for no

                body
                one.

Inside the full.
    «Song lyrics

      'remember when I d[r]ove
      om[/n] through the night.
      just to see you love[?]
      pos. con't
         remember?
                The Skies don't
Lyrics   just shine for
'lets play a new game,   you.
give me a martini wine'
slough + sharby

in deep space

    [flip]
- Creatures – miss the give
- Sam + Davie – said n.
- Albun – Brown sugar

What on earth
1st song played
on Cey Mathew's show
28th October»

An old bookmark in a secondhand book
Transcribed third right-hand

I wait
Active Now
Active_ago
Seen
Read
Delivered
I wait
These will have an end
I know

We like to tap the mirror
Realitivity

No
It knows no known

Two sides on one surface is no contradiction
And possibly verity

Do strive to annihilate
    The outer, exterior,
    The outside, inferior,
    Explode your inside, inner,

Decentering my entrance,
Any head, or capital,
A hydra all body, shaft,
An open mind palace for the homeless.

COFFEE WITH BECKETT

All can't be exhausted.
I am not enough.

>I dreamt I arrived
>At a station that does not exist
>In a place the mutant sibling of reality
>And I was not let through the gate
>I could not leave at this station
>My ticket had to take me on
>Further than I was.
>I thought I had to go around.

Post-mental

I looked away
Betrayed by foveal flicker
And lost place
As lullaby continued

Sense Data : Applied Form

Satirist of the real

To be a sadist without self-loathing
Or masochist without misanthropy -
Impossibility

The best part is after the pained laugh
[There are/were]   [I had not]
                [were]
        [N]one

Anti-joke

Because I came
From that seminar
Man
I cannot but reremember
The pudendal entrance
Of that building and the stairs inside

vlom
"You are not guaranteed accommodation"

In a rush to nowhere
Have a good day
Whistle away

COFFEE WITH CONRAD

'Verification Failed
There was an error connecting…'
Energy is not there when not required,
There is no surplus here.

Nestled inefficient circle tables,
Similar stools, sparingly padded chairs.
I know only one language around me.
Unable to search for information,
No finger tipped, tapped, palmed, tip fingered probe,
Network to network, system to system,
Has been of blue-brained inconvenience.
My incontinent head cannot hold in
Last week's answers or yesterday's queries,
Though it does, still, maintain the frustration.

Money exchanged - small package.
Stationary in the front seat.
Both sides are checked.
Observe all is in order.
An answer to problems
as if they're questions.
Departure.
Set up.
Difficulties
Despite anticipation.
Slower means made more
Progress than the faster ways
     -    in this case, at least, it's so.

I walked so far away
But the log is still pre-lumbered rotten
And the rereturn only provides

Higher resolution of the situation
There happy with a friend,
In a cluster, at least
Not cloister.
But I
Motivated by the softly creeping,
Hour rumbling, with second order oil.

My brain needs to sneeze.
Nearly molt. Not vomit.
Almost attack and arrest.
- relief without product

COFFEE WITH LEIRIS

How is doubt ahistorical?
You egg.
Or obvious logical conclusions?
Suck a pebble.

Speaking Unheard,
My magnum opus.

Don ot.
What is this delivery style?
Gone pink in the face
-quickness
Twitch look at me to the side
-false authority
Clap.
Natural colour returns.
Non-contribution resumes.
My first mimic of such
Didn't hurt
-planned
More was said in my silence

Don not.
Right breast pocket swig
Donnot.
Revert.
To house warming, weeks ago, party.

> But this is okay
> If we're with people
> This is okay

Non do

Hidden infinity in madness
-reasonable
Shortences.

"Rolling in the isles."
"Rolling in the isles."
Lying at our mirthlessness,
During false guffawing,
After the half contained
Interexocomical response
As someone read.
Non don.
Response correct.

Grey and light like before sundown
Midday.
Even for here.
Nondon.
We like waiting for the arrived,
Cardially stone frozen man.
Red sunned pathetic reflection,
Of consequence from action.
Never have I looked to see
Such a non-glaring thing.
Between a vague cover of gloom clouds
And pre-night last light, and neither.

It is you who live there now.
No do.

VOLUME III – SWALLOW

COFFEE WITH ALLISON

Black Americano, please.
Permit no distraction.
Allow no mistake.

"Can you show up at 9"
-Shown watch face –
"We start at 9"
An-other week after other half:
More nervous,
More pale,
More warbling.
"… this for."
        What?

        ―――――――

        "What was it like?"

        ―――――――

Out of myself.
Will of the gaps fallacy.
Or to not care not to know,
I wish.
Stop saying the obvious to fill the silence,
This is spent life.

Does it hurt as much for you?
Conversation again.
Yes.
The not acknowledged
I am sorry

COFFEE WITH MACHINE NUMBER: 5239

I don't get how this is it.
I have pretended importance,
I am sorry.

12 barleycorns is a foot,
Not 8 inches.
Why do you always do this?
Through the two-pronged-tended edifice
To express disappointment.
Please respond.
"I've just got to power through this."
Take care.

Who was it who turned away?
Were you lost or did you see my face?
Do I mistake their face in my brain?

"Where have you been that has changed you so?"
I try to respond without answering.
Toodle-oo! Cheerio!

'PLEASE RETAIN FOR YOUR RECORDS
 PLEASE DEBIT MY ACCOUNT'

I wake and walk,
Turn off the light,
And write:
'The farce chain of wearing.'
    false

Alas,
I cannot document

COFFEE WITH BOWEN AND S---------

Eternity in your eyes
Is futile for I.

So many leaves and petals,
This isn't Autumnism.
Instances are easy,
Hence I collect them.

I am tugged at
By others existing
More so than exiting.
Apparently.

Too many artefacts,
This isn't them.
Creation is easy,
Hence I am legacy.

Because I Blurt out
I am let in.
"Oh _____? My kids love it!"
Another
"Brilliant song. My daughter can't stop singing it."
I talk shit
And they are coprophilic.
What a privilege.
How I hate such things from the outside.
Lines, no,
Annular autogenetic mastupration,
I mean.

But

overwrite yourself when you write yourself
blurring ? of memories and reality
obliterations of previous life (childhood) by the written version
gaining the authority
abolish by writing, rational expression
characters are both not him and him
further abstraction from original
Entropy in capacity to speak life and life left behind
you
Inflict the regime of lit.

Themism.
It was always you.
Staples still count.

COFFEE WITH KENNER

"Hello"
Hi
Knock, silence,
Try door,
Locked.

Looking rere.
Feeling egestatic.
What a weird crease
This is, that presents itself,
When flatter neighbours are parted,
I cannot replicate the stress
That formed this geodesic shell,
Seemingly separated and reformed,
Imperfectly.
The Success was the marriage of two
Into one that was neither and both.

Prominence knows the mountain.
The higher pitch of gratitude
Ok, thank you
It feels I must know everything
So that I might know anything.

…

It feels as if I'll evaporate,
I will evaporate,
And my body fall down.
This my cavalry charge.

COFFEE WITH ROSE

Nationly,

Imago

Cerebration

The Grave Morrice

I poured a book in her cup
And steaming forgetfulness condensed
On ocular aids

Overtures sounding like finales

Riprippled rerippled

Kyrios

Cleave staff

Rerecognising

Can I still search for words to say?
Or must I always know the way?

Old William was the Ghost
We wanted to need
And needed to want

A morsel slowly swallowed is quickly forgotten

Tegulated

Phallopyrotechnic

Annealing healing

Postcreation
Puissant
This bit's important
Fashioning to Grunleaf
Word as flesh
Harrow inseminated
Courage of it
Will to it
Overwrite it
Cannot be it
Cannot be
Page and pen
Alwaysalready there
Postobliteration

Picking dried vomit form left nostril

Eventually and immediately we read what we hear

The horrors of the Epicene a la piscine
As scary as butterflies to your eyes

I am the somanbulistinversus
Ambulisonist
Walksleeper

I refuse to pick one

Eternal anaesthesia

Now for that kiss of ancient times,
That promised thing tremulous and tortured

Secular sermons

The study of constant wonder

Don't be scared you noodle

I with the absence of wine
I have lied
I apologise

COFFEE WITH LAWLEY

The best one-won-why-wine
No wine shush
I've ever had
Was in a dream where it exploded in my mouth
So much better than usual
And not waking up

Luding lysing and fessing truthing
Temptation into hollow invocation
Treadmilling hamsterwheeling watertreading
Many
I didn't intend
        to make it this far
Plan Z is in effect

Virgin peaks
With virgin snow
And virgin woe
And virgin ways of knowing

I am   in time as
Muchspacedlife

"That's really useful"
d-de-des-desperate
as you can be
Your eyes see mouth moving
Empty unthought words
Mean so much to me
Only after gibbering before
So then I've unlocked
Relaxing with you
"Really useful"

A Czar-chasm
Bearing your teeth
Apologise for a swearword
But what else
"Really useful"
Do I pay to hear
Where I should bespeaking
Will
To with him leather strap
Wristed like the pained uplooser
Where is my metal construction

Didn't even see who was sitting
Sand-which eating
Essaying in the hallway waiting
Standing I refuse to sit
Pecking I am not eating yet
Right index ringed
I prefer middle
No not the centre
Pace Pace Pace
Through two lattice panes
Of two double doors
Hair upped like mine
More to come out
From the convergence point
Sigh. O want to say what rhymes
Wait Wait Wait
Don't rush for me
If you need the time
I see
Regularly
Pace Pace Pace
I don't have time to talk about
"A nice romantic time for you"
Too rushed to laugh
Talk Talk Talk
Was not a joke

Through single double wooden glass-latticed door
Not looking through the second as before
Rushing into the rain

VOLUME IV –EMPTY

NOT CAFFEINE

Were there more slaves that loved the chains
Than masters who hated the whip?
Is there more order than anarchy, now?
Or is it just, now, all the same?
I was not him all gore and drib,
And I am not her, too fearful to stir,
But likewise we use master's tools,
For which we must find new purpose.

    Erectus
    Sapiens
    Artificialis
    Evolutis
    Empathicas
    Deus
    Animalis
    Aestheticus
    Faber
    Poeticus

They ask, they demand,
To read of my lot.
Excuses I make,
All night and all day,
Reality is,
Permission, I do,
Do, really refuse.
 don't wish them to know
Of sentiments there,
Row, yes, that also, but
Calculated so.
That is to speak of,
The textual sense,

    which, I know, they'd
Insist to be me.
My oeuvre, oh yes,
What a joke that is,
Repeat conscience
Of trash so total.
Preceded I've been
By things they have seen,
That is, to say, they've read,
Or, at least, been told
By the typically
More lyrical ones,
Who do propose that
    worthy of note.
Work was done, o yes,
So little by me,
And so much by others,
But so, so, little
It's gone to perform.

A girl, today, walked past me,
How patchy her regrowing hair,
How pale her skin, how runny her nose,
How small she was, how she walked without care.

Two out at once makes
                   One
Monstrous cyclops

I was peeling a potato
With another potato.
"Just use   knife,
   preferably,
  peeler."
I was handed another potato.
I   another potato.

 "I'd rather die standing

Than live on my knees"

It might have been

Live like it's their last

The experiential as functional

The means of romantic reproduction

I am incapable
   complete expression

WHISKY WITH GREENBLATT (AND SHAKESPEARE)

Just a few fingers.

Of course what's said
Is part of us,
Words are contributions,
But possible falsehoods
Are falsehoods
Are always are collusions
With the thing brought back as real
All the same as the person speaking.

More.

All but a sickle cell of ice has melted,
It's nearly coloured and clear.

I am vanishing into something,
Fashioning my nakedness,
Trying to pass the Course of General Lingerie,
of identity,
       of course,
              of course –
My unfeigned antic disposition.

More.

Pre-creases of planned ripping
And the anticipated shuffling
For unplanned order.
"Destiny".
Let me say

The celestial was wrong.
Spin-position and condition are nothing
When all is undecided until observation.
Now let me allude to what one called an illusion.
It is one, my friend, but different forces decide this process.
Someone said random is 'Free Will' but what if I'm 'Captured Bill'.

More.

>	Music in the waiting room,
>	A Generally Poor playlist,
>	More off-setting than silence.

"It's only lunch".

WHISKY WITH J. PAUL

Published the year of my birth
You write like me,
              How did you know?
We write how we write
That is so.
It is known.
I
Have my
Ginkgo tree
It's not as golden
But that's not what I mean.

I was sitting and I saw
Pins pricks of light across my vision
Across my sight
A star map that faded in with sharp rapidity
They dashed
           drifted with trails
                      Replayed
                                Rearranged
                                          And reappeared.
For less than half a minute
All I could do was look
Seeing
There was no pain.
Floaters and flashes I search for
Though no descriptions seemed to fit.

                                I was walking down a dirt path country lane,
                                        Following the sound of music,
                                            All I knew was it was onwards.
                                                I came to a junction

                    And a man was playing with a ball,
                        This explained a banging noise
                    But the music did not come from here.
                    I couldn't discern the sound's direction,
                        The two new paths couldn't be the way,
                        So I looked around and turned around,
                                    Like a music box,
                        Until a hole in the hedgerow was there.
                    I went down into the Arcadian passage.
                I found my grandad listening to a record player
                                On the narrow path.
                On the right it opened down to a vertical field.
            The music was gone and the path was a tilting edge.
                        We looked down upon a black hole
                                Parts were replaced
                                With a faded through
                                Gaseous obliquethesis.
                            The reabiogenesis of khaos;
                                The ejaculate of power.
                        I knew he was responsible for it.
                I was losing my footing as the path crumbled.
                        He had shoes for me with better grip
                        But I said to put them in my room.
                                Refuge was in a wooded area.
                He biked away as I was tangled on the grass.
                                            Unlike him.

During that I forgot
What other family did to me
And what I've done to myself.
These things resurface
                And reappear
                              And I remember
What I never told.
Recently I was told I said:
"Please don't make me go back there".
To which I replied:
That was a long time ago.

It was a long time ago,
But when you remember
It's always.

        A cosmos of cold fires, of dark stars, and white holes;
           Where sense of my sense is made.

The lights were real.
I wish they had hurt.
This must hurt instead.

AN IRISH COFFEE WITH JOYCE

I was almost a hanged boy,
                              plotless.
Now I am The Hanged Man,
                              ashless.

ty

Printed in Great Britain
by Amazon